MW01243968

Copyright © 2021 Shalisha Cook

All rights reserved. No part of this publication may be reproduced or distributed in any form, or by any electronic or mechanical methods—except in the case of brief quotations embedded in articles and reviews—without written permission from its publisher.

ISBN: 9798764214641

Book Design by Ezenwa W.
First Edition 2021
Published in the United States

DECLARATION OF LOVE

Love comes in many forms and with it comes many lessons and experiences that redefine the way we view ourselves, partners, friends, family, and the world.

It is my hope that this work allows for reflection and resonation, while providing healing. There is beauty in the darkness and light that we hide away from the world in order to survive. True self-love comes from facing our internal struggles and allowing them to be unearthed, felt, accepted, forgiven, and released to make space. A shift is imminent, groundbreaking and painful. There is so much beauty in it all at once. Self-love and self-care is a revolutionary act of kindness.

FOREWORD

by Rukiya Bluford

I remember being on a self-growth retreat with Shalisha and our peer ed group where we were introduced to the mask exercise. In pairs, we took turns layering papier-mâché on each other's faces and allowed them to dry before turning them into a version of the everyday masks we wear in our real lives.

It can be natural to want to fit in to the world around us; what becomes unnatural is when we lose or hide parts of ourselves that aren't as accepted. When we have to bury trauma, secrets, and grief under strength, resiliency, and often humor. These masks shape and form the way we survive and live amongst our family, friends, and communities. In turn, they end up shaping us and who we think we should be.

For me, to purge the mask is to align with parts of yourself that feel unlovable, uncomfortable, and unreachable. Is it to break up generations of foot-on-the-neck oppression and give voice to parts of you that were meant to stand out. Purging is healing, unapologetic, and raw. And the mask is there to hold you together until you can hold yourself fully.

After reading her first publication, *Botanicals for the Black Soul*, it has been an honor to read *Purging the Mask* and connect with that journey of becoming our authentic selves.

Table of Contents

The Cycle

The sadness is real.
It's so strong that it starts to seep through my insides
and pour through my eyelids,
weakening the barriers that made me ice.
Consuming my thoughts and telling me,
"You not good enough."

So thick that I can hardly breathe
and my heart feels as if it's seconds from bursting out my chest.

I get the feeling this happened before and it'll continue.
The rejection eats at my very soul,
trapping my being in a molded existence.
Crying silently through the rage to displace my heartbreak,
the love I strived for
constantly dangled out of my reach.

They never failed to tell me I'm not worthy.

One's drugs consumed their being
and desecrated the very appearance of normalcy,
while the other bruised me with words and rained down beatings
with objects to replace belts and fists.

Why?
I used to cry.
All I wanted was their love.
To be seen.
To be heard.

But nobody sees me.
My identity distorted to fit their satisfaction.
Now I'm stressed and hurt,
blocking out the beauty of being me.
Smiling to hide the sadness no longer suits me
and the equivalents of my parents seemed to invade my dreams.

I cried Today

I cried today
The most I've cried in weeks
Because my mind has been saying that
life would be better without me
That my broken dreams sowed my soul
a penance I can't keep
And I'm fighting my other side that hides deep within
telling me to carve signs in my skin

I cried today
Like a newborn calling to its mother
In my sheets lay a darkness,
easing up my spine and paralyzing my voice
While those hands held my vision hostage
and caressed me like a fiddle

I cried today
Remembering the ways his eyes replaced mine
My fist ached as I punched in the full-length mirror

Me Too

It happened to Me Too

At the tender age of 3,
he'd call me into his room
My fear littered the sheets
like blood from open wounds
His fingers strummed me open,
stealing my innocence

It happened to Me Too

Warm hands covering my mouth,
as he explored me
Leaving me disgusted
as my stomach churned inside out
from unwanted kisses on my cheek
In my mind, I resigned that
nobody would ever want me

It happened to Me Too

During the dark of the night,
so my insomnia passes with the sunrise
And my oversized clothes
override the internal sunshine
that once filled my child eyes

It happened to Me Too

Yet they called me a liar,
igniting a fire of disbelief in me
So my soul grew cold
as these stained my face
Because it happened to

Me Too

Resilient Voices

Their voices carried them
as their feet bled into the pavement
Mentally, the shackles had taken their toll
leaving them with no way out
This was what we became
as we filled a boat with our bodies
Men and women sacrificed themselves
Birthing a new terror in the ocean
Or was it just our imaginations running away with us
from lack of nutrition

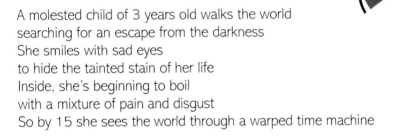

A molested child of 3 years old walks the world
searching for an escape from the darkness
She smiles with sad eyes
to hide the tainted stain of her life
Inside, she's beginning to boil
with a mixture of pain and disgust
So by 15 she sees the world through a warped time machine

Her ancestors survived slavery
Her brother survived rape
So she assumes that she can survive her dirty secret
What are we, if not survivors?
The hands we've been dealt built our resilience,
yet our voices they couldn't take

The Journey

I wondered if I could conquer the world
and in some ways
it's inevitable.
But then my heart assured my mind
that there is no such thing.

Why is it that we believe releasing our sorrows
and laying ourselves bare
is a fast track
to losing who we are.

How do we shift this?

Is it after our eyes have closed
and sadness sent us to an early death?
Or our raging war with the world
over possession of our sanity?

The legacies are written on our bodies.

Feel it.

Be bestowed with the ability to live life to the fullest.

Embrace those gifts unapologetically and be you. Be us.

That's our ascension to a better person than before

Motivated by our sadness,
we felt and transformed
so that happiness is a constant

Pieces

They were something like a sunshine
Lighting up spaces with an energy that was self-made
Yet their hearts were on a rampage
to get back the pieces that they lacked

Their minds created walls
that turned the shining sun
into daggers of discomfort

Insert the tongue-lashing, fiery assassin
hiding insecurities through manipulative tendencies

Hoping to be set free
by some unknown lover in life
But the loneliness never went away

It remained a thorn inside,
rooting love in despair
creating a karmic connection
of abandonment

Leaving them tongue-tied
in a knot of dream catchers

Masks

We sometimes forget our voices
Believing that our vulnerability
will lead us to unreasonable cracked pieces

But our screams relay
the dreams of our hearts
as we turn inside out and self destruct

We hide behind our defenses
fearing that intimacy and being seen
will expose our abandoned child that's stored away

Honestly, there is no shame
in removing our masks
and allowing our true being to shine

Simply because
it is a variation of our most intimate parts
that have been warped by worldly trauma
Yet ignored by our soul due to fear of corruption

Equals

Many people don't know,
but she shared a womb with me

Her masculinity completes my femininity
the way moths flock to flames

She was the constant
when parents were hard to come by
and straight faces spilled real lies
In ways, she's the lemon to my tequila,
the jack to my coke,
the lighter to my smoke
that eases down someone's throat

Other times, she's the vinegar to my oil,
the consistent composition of white
to my enrapturing red wine,
enough to rip tongues out of mouths,
air out of lungs,
and hearts out of chests.

Her unlabeled aggressive identity
fitting my femme visibility
like an eclipse before the new moon

The yin to my yang,
Push to my Pull
My equal

My twin

Like Them

I remember wishing that my skin
was the color of sand paper
or pale like some of my closest friends.

Internally, I envied how everyone looked at them.

They were considered desirable,
girlfriend material,
but I was not.
Many people interacted with them,
treating me like a shadow
that was good enough to exist
but not to be seen or heard.

I was the black stain
that tainted a trio of porcelain dolls
that everyone seemed to be in love with.
I cried in front of mirrors
because I didn't look like them.

Wishing that somehow
I could articulate
and smile my way into a higher standing.

Buried inside of me,
there was this hate of my melanin
that was rooted much deeper
than the fact that I could tether between
Shalisha from Camden
and Shalisha the Valedictorian.
Code switching on cue so society doesn't belittle me.

I hated me.
I hated me.
I hated me
because in this society,

I grew up knowing that
women who looked like me
had to work harder,
be smarter,
be five times as good as everyone else
and still be overlooked.

My voice would be heard
but never listened to
and that made me aspire to be someone else.
A person that was a lot less black, brown,
or any feature that made me less "Beautiful".

Funny.

Cause overtime,
 became blacker,
hair kinkier,
my vibe more unapologetic
and my true beauty shining through.

My blackness
needed to be loved
and celebrated by me.

No need to be lighter
or have whiter features
to be loved by the outside world.

Seriously, I could never be like them.

Run

Run
Run Run
Run Run Run

Run
Like your life depends on it
Even as chests heave searching for oxygen
There is no owner of accomplishments
Lying in wait for compensation
You have cried and bled a condensation
Large enough it floods acidic

How many feet whipped backs spun a joyous exclamation,
While the hooded darkness
aligned chakras to resemble a crooked staircase?
Did you survive it?

Forgetting that the pain ran up roots
Stunting trees in seamless stages
A dull reminder churns every time you look at him
Fear coiling inward when the memories surface
It never was sounded the infectious lies

Your Brilliance made you coachable
Shortly reshaped and renamed an uppity arrogance
Consumed is your identity of this nonsense
Waterfalls to stream endlessly so

Run

Guilt

Guilt
I felt it the entire time we were together
It cut off my windpipe and seeped in my being

Who was I to have friends you didn't know?
How dare I have independence while having you by my side?

The guilt made me cry
It caused me to feel unworthy
I should've been grateful that someone like you
wanted me, despite my flaws

The display of your frustrations with me,
evident from the beatings I received

So I continued feeling guilty

Why couldn't I do anything right?
What made me smile
when someone other than you told me I was beautiful?

This guilt made me comply
Taking away my fight or flight

Take her back

Take her back to late night clubbin' with friends,
resulting in 1 am homebound arrivals
Now she checks in before 10 so his love remains
Yeah, those checkins turned violent

But she was in love

His demeanor sparked a flame that melted her icy cold exterior
The harsh words she'd inhale as her only lifeline
So what happens when his backhand plays smack cam
and her body stings in places that are littered with bruises?

Take her back to that Goddess confidence,
turning heads when she stepped in a room

Now she's self conscious

Praying for No
standing out but blending in
to fit in and dodging attention

Her beauty that drew him in,
made him decide she'd be his love in this lifetime
Now it's demonized cause he feels she only needs to be seen by him

Those insults leave her distraught
She's fighting to stay alive
after he assumed she's telling lies
on why someone looked her in her eyes

Is this love?

Becoming someone's punching bag
and forgetting the self-love you had
Cause the bruises are elusive
and accepting don't mean exclusive

Anchor

They told me I was their Anchor,
keeping them afloat in this stream of emotion
That notion should've warned me
Cause no breast stroke makes the dead float
This boat I am sailing is an honest inflection stopping my blessings
My strength keeping us in balance
and not once did they offer solace
No comfort was found in doing the work for both of us
Our souls searching for wholeness
but the process forced me to counterproduce
Used and emotionally abused, I held on to be your lifeline
But in due time, you showed me that anchors are expendable

Late Night Dawn

Talking to you on those late nights
I used to feel like everyday was date night
Cause my thoughts would ease the time personified like dotted lines
And the deepest part of you made the moon light
Our conversations revealed the pain we hide
while the quality of our time made me sing inside
You became my late night inspiration and confider of my sins
so my confidence in you never prepared me for our end
I agreed, simply caused there's no point in begging another
The loneliness I felt, made me sit down and wonder
Should I have cried from deep inside, begged, asked you why
or caused a scene to assume accountability
But I was sure that I had been the best me
Bringing vulnerability so your feelings were held dear
and your energy cleared
Now my eyes are leaking cause my heart is torn to pieces
but I remember
Life moves on cause the darkest nights always meet the dawn

Together again

My love is something close to my heart
I gave it to you cause you said you'd cherish the spark
Reality, you got what you want by tearing it up
Why should I allow you a second chance?
You told ya lies, played your games, now your ass is banned
On higher ground, I can see who you are
Promise you'd never leave me,
turned around and beat me,
packaged up my love and walked out the door
Betrayal, everytime my face met the back of your hand
Somehow, I still yearned to be together again

Untitled

There was something about the way you spoke to me
Imprinting on my soul like loose leaf in a cool breeze
We seemed to shift extremes without the thought of insecurities
You shone like the one
Gleaming as a diamond in a coal sea

Soul Language

Look into her eyes past the intensity
Can you tell that she smiles through her pain?
Do you feel how much loneliness fills her heart?
How many times have those eyes bewitched you?
Leading you on like a piper with its python
So like storm, her eyes change the weather
The brighter the irises the happier she is internally
A dull smoke cloud bleeding to the surface,
pulling you in unexpectedly
Subtle warning that you should beware
Pause.
Look me in the eyes.
Make eye contact.
It's the only way you'll understand a woman like me
This gateway to my soul speaks a sacred language

Before the Spring

Falling in Love, I thought she was the right one for me
But now, I see she satisfied a few of my requirements
Cause I was blinded by the bonding time
Peeling back the facade,
she seemed to internalize the worse parts for me
But never could she love what she couldn't see
Those hopeful dreams grew weak, weathering like dying leaves
And she left me before the start of Spring

We planned our wedding and the timeline for our offspring
Wanting them to have more than the things we'd seen
So when she asked to downgrade this,
I knew that I didn't want to revisit a love like this
Where I was loving on my own, holding us afloat,
and assuring that the both of us would grow
It was a lesson not to settle for those emotionally unavailable
Reminding me that I deserve a love that's free,
where I'm treated as a Queen
I'm grateful that she left me before the Spring

Empty Seams

Expectation met with disappointment,
used to bring out the hurt in me
Holding loved ones hostage,
hoping not to set them free

I believed that they should've accept the best of me,
ignoring all my empty seams, never calling me out on things
Unconsciously intimidating them into discomfort,
allowing selfish oblivion but then again
the loneliness spoke louder than my cynicism

Sweet memories overshadowed as I lashed out,
creating doubt cause I wouldn't let the past drought
That victim mentality leaving no space to breathe so
 would digress to dissect what I refused to see

AFTERWORD

by Rukiya Bluford

I remember being on a self-growth retreat with Shalisha and our peer ed group where we were introduced to the mask exercise. In pairs, we took turns layering papier-mâché on each other's faces and allowed them to dry before turning them into a version of the everyday masks we wear in our real lives.

It can be natural to want to fit in to the world around us; what becomes unnatural is when we lose or hide parts of ourselves that aren't as accepted. When we have to bury trauma, secrets, and grief under strength, resiliency, and often humor. These masks shape and form the way we survive and live amongst our family, friends, and communities. In turn, they end up shaping us and who we think we should be.

For me, to purge the mask is to align with parts of yourself that feel unlovable, uncomfortable, and unreachable. Is it to break up generations of foot-on-the-neck oppression and give voice to parts of you that were meant to stand out. Purging is healing, unapologetic, and raw. And the mask is there to hold you together until you can hold yourself fully.

After reading her first publication, *Botanicals for the Black Soul*, it has been an honor to read *Purging the Mask* and connect with that journey of becoming our authentic selves.